D1516186

CAPSULE STORIES

Spring 2020 Edition

Published exclusively by Capsule Stories

Contents

Letters from the Editors

Rain means so many different things to different people. Even to me, it depends what state of mind I'm in for how it affects me. Sometimes, rain can be cleansing. It has the power to wash away my burdens and serves as a cosmic sign that whatever I'm holding on to is best let go. Other times, rain is an excuse to stay home and get cozy with a book. Sometimes rain understands my despair better than my therapist can. Rain can mean whatever you want it to be. But one thing's for sure: rain, in all the meaning we ascribe to it, is worth writing about.

—Natasha Lioe, Founder and Publisher

Wait until a dark, stormy night when you just can't fall asleep, sneak out to your favorite chair or couch, and read this edition by lamplight as the rain pounds against the window. Experience life's cleansing rains and blustery storms with these writers, and feel what they feel. Feel the raindrop balancing on your fingertip; feel the expectant energy the storm brings; feel the weariness of staying up all night, unable to sleep. We hope you enjoy this Spring 2020 Edition of *Capsule Stories* and the wonderful works these writers contributed.

—Carolina VonKampen, Publisher and Editor in Chief

Sleepless Rainy Nights

You hear the droplets splatter on the ground, first once, then again, then a million times over, making music like only nature can. Rain hits your windshield on your way to work. Your jacket clings to your skin. Socks soaked through. Books soggy around the edges. The trees sway above you, but you're afraid to look up at the sky—angry, sad, romantic, calming. All at once. With no sign of it ending.

The rain distorts the world around you, your eyes peering through windows that only show your reflection, tears streaming down the face that peers back at you. Your head on a pillow, staring up at the ceiling, wondering when the silence will come.

In the morning, you wake up and it's gone. The trees stand a little taller, the grass a little longer; the driveway is still wet. The storm is over, but the world remembers.

Droplets

Niamh McNally

Droplets

burst
near your ears

refreshing spumes
of March mist

between city gulls
and chimney cliffs

clinging to lashes
blurring the view

every layer
drenched through

a not so innocent

drizzle

Ode to a Rainstorm

Benjamin Middendorf

Originally published in *Potpourri 2017*

I.
As I drift up out of sleep,
the remnants of a dream slipping away,
I hear its soundtrack repeated
outside my window.
The soft, metallic rap on the air conditioner,
the liquid burble of erosion in microcosm.
It's raining this morning. I hadn't thought
to check the forecast
and was rewarded by the surprise.
The best rain might be that which comes
out of nowhere, for it can never disappoint
with claims of monsoon-ity, of lasting for eons.
It just is
a gift to my morning.

II.
That is not to say that midnight rain
does not hold its joys,
for more often than not it comes
accompanied by the breaths of the trees
exhaling in long gasps.
The warning grunt echoes
from the Mississippi, and I wait
for it to inch closer, the sound and sights
that brought to mind sportive gods
for the ancients. The storm was a destructive
tantrum. Not so to me.
Each flash of splintered air is entirely planned
with forethought for its effect on those below.

The boom of bass, the risky scent of melted sky
is a concert created for those of us
who like to sit on the step
and watch.

III.
Yet I've never experienced a rain that overreaches itself,
spilling into basements and raising up old memories
of a family's heritage.
The quilt stitched by grandma, photos of grandma, grandma's
corpse,
all shaken from their rest and brought floating
into the open air, utterly
wrecked.
I've never experienced the rain
that waits like an Irrigated Effluent Damp,
taking your tire and throwing it
against the guardrail and over.
God's first chosen tool of extermination
was not fire and brimstone, earthquakes, or plagues.
It was a drop of water. Followed by another. And another.
Until the planks of a single boat creaked and groaned
under the pressure of salvation.

IV.
And yet, despite the floods,
I cannot temper my love for moisture.
The scent of fermenting leaves has for too long
been a signal of melancholy and contemplation
for me to resist it now.
The gray cadavers that line the path will never
deter my urge to splash through puddles.

The swish of a slicker brings far more aesthetic pleasure
than an umbrella. I feel every droplet,
sense the shifts in tempo or pressure,
experience the change in my fortunes.
One should not hold off time at arm's length.

V.
I long for the rain that falls in other places,
for it seems that it should be entirely different.
The rain of England smells
like castle mortar and Earl Grey.
The shower of the Amazon like sharp leaves
and the moldering coats of sloths.
I would enjoy a rain tour. To plan a trip
with bad forecasts in mind, and then
to feel disappointed
when the sun pokes through a cloud
and melts away the fall, would be
delightfully odd.

Fishing in the Dark

Larry Griggs

When I was younger, I lay awake at night, sweating in the heat of summer. I gripped the blanket tightly over my head, preparing to be taken. There's an unspoken rule that if you pull the blanket over your head at night the monsters can't get to you. They would be waiting though, in the darkness of the closet, when you thought you were safe. I didn't understand why I was acting so irrational; anxiety, the therapists at my school had said.

Sleep had finally come when my father nudges me awake with the sole of his boot. Although my brain is still groggy, I can tell that he smells of cigarette smoke and malt liquor.

"Go get in the car," he slurs, leaning on the door frame for support.

He keeps the light off as I pull on pants, and after I put on my shoes he hurries me out of the house. It's raining hard when we go outside. The rain pelts my shirt as I run to the passenger side door and wait until he unlocks the door. He drops his keys once, twice, and finally opens the door and lets me in. I'm shivering by the time I clamber into the seat and put on my seatbelt. My dad turns on the heat when he notices my soaked T-shirt, then puts the car in drive. We coast down the driveway with the lights off, and when we reach the road, he flips on the lights and guns the engine. We drive down a dark road in silence, the only sound coming from the radio that plays an old R&B song over the platter of rain on the car. My father lights a cigarette, and I slink down in the seat and turn my head to the side, trying to find a small pocket of clean air. He turns abruptly and parks the car on the bank of a hill. I watch him as he stares blankly ahead for a few moments, and then he reaches over and opens the glove compartment.

It drops like my mouth because sitting in the glove box is a revolver longer than my arm. *Well this is it,* I think. *I'm gone.* I tense up, but my father reaches around the gun and grabs a fishing hook. He holds it up so I can see and smiles. From what I can see, there's nothing special about it. It's a simple lure, a rainbow-colored elongated oval that sprouts a hook at the end. He told me once that it was his luckiest one. He'd caught the slimy-looking catfish with whiskers that we have in the living room with it. It was the biggest fish that he had caught and not immediately eaten afterward. He then rushes out of the car, and I hear the trunk open and feel the force slam against the car when he shuts it. I'm still confused as I watch through the rain-streaked window as my father begins to fish. His hat flies off and his shirt ripples in the wind. He struggles to cast a line without the wind ripping the fishing pole from his hands. At one point, he falls over right into the bank of the lake. His body is still for a moment and for a second I feel tempted to go out and help him, but he pulls himself up and his body is shaking. At first I think it's because he is cold, but I realize that this man is *laughing.* He struggles to fish for a few more minutes, yelling defiantly to the wind before he runs back to the car. He's covered in dirt and straw, dripping wet.

"Did you catch anything?" I ask.

He shakes his head no, but the smile still hasn't left his face. He reaches behind him and grabs a can of beanie weenies. He opens the top with a pocketknife and grabs a spoon from his backseat. He takes a few bites then hands the can to me. I take the can and take a few bites like he had done and hand the can back. We do this until the can is empty, and he promptly throws the can out of the window.

He wipes his mouth with the back of his hand and turns

to me and says, "There is no better feeling than fishing in the dark. Remember that."

I nod. I didn't know what else to do in that moment. He starts the car again, allowing me to pick the radio station. I put it back on the station that he had it on earlier. The rain stops a mile before we are home, taking the magic of the night with it.

Years later when my father died from a combination of cigarette smoking, red meat, and bad oral hygiene, the first task my mother completed was selling his possessions. Gone were his guns, which he had polished daily, usually in the company of my older sister's promising new boyfriends. I was given his clothes, old dress shirts and jackets that hung off my tiny frame. When it came to his car, my mother sold it for fifty dollars to one of the neighbors down the road. As she cleaned out the car later that afternoon, her hand came across the simple lure, the one with all of the luck. She looked at it with a wistful smile and before she could put it in the trash bag, I felt something open inside me, a door back to the boy I had been, timid and afraid, full of anxiety.

"Wait," I told her. "I want it."

She gave me a smile and pressed the lure in my hand. I held it up like my father had done in the car and felt nothing. I bought a case for it and placed it on the top shelf of my closet. But the sad and well-known fact of the matter is that the things we leave behind will never speak to us. It is only a totem for a memory to plant itself on. Our reasons and our regrets will never hold truth or volume, but the feelings of the moments that we share with the people that we love belong to the living, just as the wind blows in the rain. My father

never took me back to the place where he had fished. Later
that year when I started driving, I couldn't find it. It was lost
somewhere, somewhere at the beginning of chaos.

*the feelings of the moments
that we share with the people
that we love belong to the
living, just as the wind
blows in the rain*

Bullfrogs

James Croal Jackson

My mind was split in two—
there was unreality. And then you two,
David and Anna. We were on the dance floor
at Phipps Conservatory when David asked
me to be best man. When I said *hell yeah*,
an octogenarian gave his all to Daft Punk
on a dance floor that's hosted hundreds
of weddings. I was writing a screenplay
in my mind that already I have forgotten.
But it probably involved a forever love,
a lotus, and a flytrap. We went outside
to see bullfrogs, to leave the indoor heat,
and there was a chorus in the swamps,
unexpected baritones and falsettos
we could not anticipate. A cool breeze
contrasted earlier heat, and rain, and
in the end I was with my friends, singing
with bullfrogs their forever songs
that will—I hope—outlast us all.

Cascadian Spring

Juleigh Howard-Hobson

The sky is solid gray, indistinctly
Separate from the ground born mists that obscure
The land with soft white swirls. It's springtime and
The world should be green leaf and pink bud, be
Blue sky and yellow light, but it's not. More
Cloud, more fog, more rain, more cold. This is land
That holds no charm. This is a world of harsh
Temperamental reality, of mud,
Of damp, of drench, of slime, of skies never
Free of clouds, of fields never free of marsh,
Of rain that flings from leaden skies to flood
Everything for most of the year. Every
Year is exactly the same here: we get
Three months of winter, and then we get wet.

Old Farmhouse Window, In the Rain

Juleigh Howard-Hobson

Black edged, the window frames the cold wind-stirred
Rain as it pours. Drops cling to the glass, run
Down to pool at the sill. The cat extends
A paw, then quietly withdraws to lick her
Fur, unhappy with the wet. There's no sun,
Just reflections prismed as daylight ends
Watery and gathered, the drops clinging
Before they fall, unraveling themselves away
As they make riverlets, shining for brief
Moments before they disappear. Pelting
New drops replace them as they go. A stray
Shape is blown up against the glass: a leaf
That sticks and messes up the lines of rain.
Drips trickle past. The leaf blows off again.

Blow

Isabella J Mansfield

Blow you beautiful storm
You ferocity
Bend trees
Until they snap
Rip roof tiles
Storm doors
From hinges
Everything unhinged

Blow

Blow garbage
From loose cans
Blow the cans
Drive them down
Debris-covered streets
Blow umbrellas
Inside out
Like the movies

Blow

Pull power lines
To the ground
Snakes sparkling
Sparking
Whipping wildly
Leave everyone
Powerless
In the dark

Blow

Blow you tempest
You beast
Be a creature
Howl at the moonlight
Around corners
Swing the shutters
Let the windows
Rattle under the roar

Blow

Blow louder, longer
Blow lullabies
To pluviophiles
Blow directives to
Storm chasers
Be the storm
One breath ahead
Chased, never caught

Blow

be the storm

when I become your thunderstorm

Tianna G. Hansen

I ask, is a storm still beautiful and brilliant
if there is no one to witness
not a soul to dance in its raindrops
nor solid ground to absorb the flash
of lightning—stark, magnificent

the shockwaves of loving you
have electrocuted me
but left you unscathed
I lie singed, changed

unable to sleep, unable to fall
into dreams. rain batters
windowpanes and still, I resist
being lulled by the sound,
wishing I could go outside to
dance within the petrichor

thunder ripples through my bones
and I wonder if it's storming
where you are, too. I know you
think of me every time lightning
flashes outside your window.

you've always called me a thunderstorm
and you, my storm chaser. will we ever
end this waltz around each other
or remain trapped in sleepless nights
beside others, dreaming of those times
we spent wrapped together

listening to the thunder and the rain
like tears pouring down at our inevitable
parting, the thunder of our bodies joining,
the lightning, quick and bright, of our love
tumbling down from a dark sky.

dreaming of those times
we spent wrapped together

the thunder of our bodies joining
the lightning, quick and bright, of our love

A Bed under the Rains

Fabrice Poussin

Thundering rains upon the steel covers
bright streaks across the walls of shadows
and the loud crash below the leafy oak.

Heat of a summer day in early spring
the sky falls apart at first sign of exhaustion
darkness succeeds under sabers of a last sun.

Softly she rests, her gaze set on a glassy sheet
dreaming of a dance in the dead of night
energized by the lights of a puzzling heaven.

If only she could read the song of those tears
smell the kindest caress of a whiter cloud
she wonders as she touches her aching essence.

When I Am Naked

Alolika A. Dutta

When I am dressed in a shapeless linen kameez that drapes over the length of my body covering me in a deadened shade of beige while I lean toward a disorganized debilitated desk with heaps of papers notes and incomplete letters scattered across a chipped wooden surface that reeks of *stagnant* hope when I depart from your side in the middle of a sleepless night to sit at this desk cabinet doors ajar and drawers pulled out a half-written poem fluttering in a familiar pair of hands and my disheveled hair tied into a loose knot tendrils hopping off my temples and chrysanthemums blooming from my breasts a soft outline of my hunched figure in the brocade curtains and a certain *urgency* in the way my finger moves from one word to another—on such nights when I am *nothing* more than unstitched words when I am *nothing* more than a wandering poet in a one-bedroom home when I have lost my middle name my address my language to this rectangular piece of paper when these crooked sentences are my only identity and when the rain is the only sound in a room with two bodies—then at that hour in that room within that body would you make love to me?

My Body
Is a
Warehouse

Alolika A. Dutta

I store everything.
I store it within the narrow white boundaries of photo-graphs—within the unintentional picture of a woman's chikankari kameez as she brushed past me at the bazaar with-in the image of a pair of idle hands on a train to nowhere within the underlined sentences in history textbooks within the cursive handwriting scattered across the dog-eared pages of a forgotten journal within the empty envelope marked with a faint lipstick stain from when I had held it between my lips on a busy Saturday afternoon while I counted a bunch of keys to a quiet house with calendars clocks and three strangers to a letterbox with dried flowers and no letters to a rusted bicycle that smells of my childhood and a wallet filled with neatly organized currency notes that have felt the greasy palms of rickshaw wallahs and florists and vendors and child laborers selling coloring books at the traffic signal noisy coins train tickets from a year ago visiting cards and a folded letter to remind me of home a pile of books and a compact mirror to console the voyeur within—

I store everything—the sweetened taste of his tongue the smell of his body that dances on my skin for days on end the light feeling of his fingers on my nape his caramel complexion the fabric of his linen shirt that hangs from his collarbone the sound of a door opening too soon and the sight of someone reading outdoors—

I store everything—in faint ink in sepia photographs in the memory of someone's voice—I store everything as if I will never feel again—I store everything because I am too afraid to forget—

I store everything for sleepless nights when I open the warehouse empty all the shelves and search for every vision every scent every sound that reminds me of him.

every vision every scent every sound
reminds   me   of   him

Charring
Light

Karin Hedetniemi

The expectant feeling of the past few hours resolved itself with a late humid rain. I came upstairs to the landing, heard the steady pattering through the open bedroom windows, and was immediately soothed. I sat on the windowsill, inhaling the fresh damp air, comforted by the rhythm of dripping summer leaves and the sight of tiny twigs flowing in frenzied curbside currents.

Jim followed upstairs with the pup. "Mad dogs and Englishmen," he proclaimed as he walked past the bedroom door. I smiled at the pleasure of living with someone who would quote Rudyard Kipling while going about evening rituals. Someone who would write a poem, send it to my printer as a surprise, and call out that he needed me to bring him the "report." Someone who would knead his hands into a peasant's dough, stretch and smear it with homemade marinara, decorate it with basil leaves and orbs of mozzarella, step back to admire the pie's rusticity, and then call out from the kitchen: "Do you want to see a thing of beauty?" His callings-out were declarations of joy.

I heard Jim rummage in the guest room closet to fetch a sweater. "'Gunga Din,' written in 1890," he called out. A moment later, he reappeared in the doorway, leaned against the frame, and began to read the poem aloud to me from his phone. He had an intensely involved expression on his face as if he needed to transmit the importance of this work, or this ordinary moment, to the deepest part of my transcendent memory. "Din! Din! Din!"

When he finished the first stanza, Jim looked up to see if I was still paying attention. He smiled at me with tiny amused glints, then pattered back downstairs. The pup followed with her little jangling of tags and nails clicking on the wooden steps. I heard the front door open and close. He'd be out there on the porch, igniting his hand-carved pipe from a birding trip to Scotland with the chrome lighter I gave him for Christmas. He'd take a few short puffs until the bowl glowed, then settle back on the bench and turn his gaze upward to the moon, or perhaps to the top of the plum tree, sensing the presence or shape of an owl. He'd fold his left arm across his chest, holding the pipe in his right. The rain would be dripping from the eaves, hitting the rhododendron bush. Soft tendrils of smoke would weave themselves into his woolen sleeves.

Dusk melted to a shadowy blue, and clouds drifted, occasionally revealing the moon, casting pale ribbons of light on the plaster walls. I stayed perched on the windowsill, transfixed, watching the plum tree branches come alive in the night wind. I didn't understand their voodoo dance, what they were trying to tell and show me, that one night after Jim was gone, I'd be sitting on that bench, wearing that smoky wool sweater, inhaling the sweet fading scent of tobacco from its sleeves, touching tiny crystallized tears on his glasses, glinting under the moon, feeling the pup's gentle leaning, and pressing his binoculars to my eyes, trying to find the barred owl, calling out from the tree.

Nights like this
remind me of us

empty
promises

Isabella J Mansfield

Nights like this remind me of us:
all biting winds and skies that threaten
to fall in love with darkness but I know
you don't love me just like I know
those clouds are not full of rainwater

Virga

(It's Always about
How Lonely
You Are)

Isabella J Mansfield

Originally published in *White Lies in Blue Ink* (2015)

I watched the sky for lightning,
the clouds full of threats.

It started to rain, but in this heat,
it evaporated before reaching the ground.

It reminded me of you, in the ways
you never quite say what you want from me.

This Weather, Am I Right?

Isabella J Mansfield

with this
screen covered

window I can't tell
if it is raining

or just gray
it looks cold

and dark, at least my
alarm clock tells me

it is morning
I can't tell otherwise if

you want me or if you
just let me be here

and whose idea was
this anyway

to put screens on the
windows so you're just

never certain if what
you're seeing is real

everything is mom

Ada Pelonia

rain is a trigger, mostly
for thoughts that've been clutched
in one hand, afraid they'd go out
and everything goes ballistic

at night is the peak, mostly
there's cold feet rubbing against
each other, friction acting like
bicycle gears moving toward
completion of the question

what would happen if
i drop out of med school

pros overpower with such ad-
vantage, points for finally having
friends for weekend joyrides,
movie marathon buddies, dates
here and there, less /or lesser/
nosebleeds and headaches
and tissues sprawled over
my room filled with either blood
    or tears

and then there's the con
alone in gloom, waiting to be read:
    everything would be sad

Sleepless

Cassia Hameline

I often wonder to myself—sometimes, most times, at midnight or one in the morning while I'm sleepless and staring at my computer screen, alone in my one-bedroom apartment in northern Texas, in a small town 1,538 miles from the house in central New York that I consider my home—where my mother spends her nights (also alone), maybe wondering what to make for dinner, maybe wondering how many dinners she's eaten alone since her husband left, maybe wondering if she'll ever find another, better man to love, or maybe wondering if she should just get a dog—while here I am sitting on a hand-me-down wooden chair left behind by the boy who lived here before me that creaks each time I shift positions, a dog of my own sprawled, legs out like a frog, on the hardwood floor behind me so that he can be closer to our one working air conditioner that blasts cool air into this stale and musty living room and slows the beads of sweat that drip down my bare back (because I'm rarely not naked now that I live alone) but not before they fall off my sweat-sticky skin onto the wooden chair that wasn't mine but now is, which I'm slumped onto, overheated, exhausted yet unable to sleep, while I listen to the dog's breaths, heavy, labored, and when I turn to look at him I smile at the way his body moves in a place only he can see, and I hurt, too, remembering the places I used to see but cannot anymore, because I left that time that place that life looking for one that could fill the holes made in me by a man I thought was good, but it hurts to hurt like this, alone in a one-bedroom apartment so far from home, so I focus on the dog's paws instead, focus on his ears on his snout on his belly that puffs in and out as he dreams; maybe of splashing through rivers back east with the neighbor's dog, Lilly, or

maybe of dashing and darting through dense pinewood for-
ests as the sun winds down for the day, or maybe he's hot on
the trail of a rabbit he just caught chewing cherries off the
bush outside our home, or maybe he's just running for no rea-
son at all; and it's the way that he puffs out brief bursts of air,
which lift his lips just slightly, and it's the way that he lets out
the smallest yelps that make him sound like a baby bird, and
it's the way that his nose flares so faintly with each dreamed
breath, and it's the way that his paws pulse to the same rapid
beat of his little dog heart, getting faster and faster and faster
and faster with each romp or river or rabbit or pine tree he
passes in this dream that keeps going for what feels like hours
but is really just two minutes, yet by the time it's over he's
tired, we're tired, he's waking up, in this one-bedroom apartment in northern Texas, where the cool air blasting my naked
back is the only thing that I want to feel, and it's nights like
these, alone, in a house, not home, searching for ways to fix
the hurt that holds me hostage but failing, fighting, fatigued
and I wonder—what is left to dream of?

what is left to dream of?

Dark Matters

Kushal Poddar

"Park your darkness in the dreams."
You know how a cloud gets away with
such statements when it rains.

When it rains the next door's rebel cabal
runs away ringing our doorbell.
Although the outdoor has darkened,
we know it is daytime.

It is daytime. A dove coos from nowhere.
Dreams purr from the dark alleys.
Everyone's doorbell rings. No one's door opens.

the
prescription

Lee Clark Zumpe

she carries the prescription
around in her purse for weeks,
the handwriting
no more legible than the musings
she scratches in notebooks
for friends and family to find
hours too   late

they told her at the clinic it would help
her stay   focused

she can't afford both medicine and cigarettes,
though,
so she grits her teeth,
takes another   drag
and opts to kill herself
ever so   slowly
instead of save herself one day
at a   time

Thinking of You

Lola Gaztañaga Baggen

---

3 a.m. Damp sheets and soft, heavy breathing, as I think of you, and me, and turn my linen into shackles. Rain hums softly in the background, trembles through the windows and walls of my small apartment; my skin; my flesh. White noise, which has never helped me sleep. It used to help you, though. You listened to recordings every night: soft, gentle rain scattered by branches and leaves, hard, sharp jabs on tin roofs, cracking thunder and roaring storms. Every night, the sound of water lulled you to peaceful slumber, helped you flee the thoughts that plagued you, the thoughts you wouldn't share. Not with me.

I can't sleep when it rains, not anymore. Gray-blue shadows shift across the faded wallpaper and form odd, distorted lines in my bedroom. The curtains are rubbish, useless against the insistent light of the moon outside, and the streetlights and neon signs, glaring and intrusive, and I find myself precariously balancing between light and dark.

Soft patter, a rush of wind, the shifting beams of light of a passing car. How do people do it? I chase for sleep like a dog chases its tail, tossing and turning endlessly. It's like forgetting how to tie your shoes if you think about it too much, or the lyrics of your favorite song, stuck on the tip of your tongue. You used to hate my tossing and turning, the way nightmares made me stick my legs out and feverishly swat away invisible ghosts that just so happened to perch on your head. I never noticed, woke up fresh as a daisy and none the wiser, until you woke up as well and bemoaned your fate as bed-companion to the world's least famous kickboxer. Your eyes would twinkle and shine as you teased me, almost enough to hide the dark circles underneath.

I tangle my toes in the bedsheets and kick out angrily, trying to wriggle free from the heavy duvet the way I'd seen a piglet flee an overbearing sow, back on my da's farm. It's hot; my sweat drips down my limbs, seeps into the mattress. Hot, and stifling, and stale. Everything in this damned city is stale. The busy subway, the tall buildings, the permeating stench of sweat and humanity—I hate every square inch of it all. We'd moved here because of your job, because of opportunities and chances, and my desire to support you. What am I still doing here?

3:45 now. Time drips down like honey; sometimes sticky and slow, sometimes mercilessly runny. Always golden, yellow, edible—that doesn't make any damn sense. Time isn't edible, or yellow. It's hard to make sense, and my thoughts skitter along the edges of the room like cockroaches, disorganized and odd. Multicolored, monochrome cockroaches. Like I'm losing my fucking mind.

Is this what you felt like?

I think of our first date, running along the pier caught in the rain. You laughed, absolutely soaked, water running down along your skin as if it wanted you as much as I did. I think of sleepless nights in my childhood, full of fretful tossing and fearful shivering as I tried to hide from the storms outside. I think of your hands pushing up underneath my shirt in the back of your car, gripping and ripping and tearing me to pieces as you made me whole, and the metallic drumming of water on the roof. I think of quiet mornings with a cup of tea and canceled outdoor plans, and painful appointments at the OB-GYN and the fertility clinic with the big, glazed-over windows that blurred out all details but the endless outpour—and thinking that the sky was crying for me.

I'd thought that that was as much pain as anyone could

---

ever feel. Then, the storm clouds I'd feared since I was a little girl grew darker and darker in your brain. Silently, quietly, sneakily. They rained and rained, and waterlogged your brain, and then they proved me wronger than I ever thought I could be.

3:50 a.m. I tear my eyes away from the glaring red lines of my alarm clock and stare up at the ceiling, gray-blue like the rest of it all, and try to tell myself what you would, if you still could.

Everything is wet, and hot, and I realize I can't breathe. The walls of the room are lined with boxes, full of memories and belongings; boxes full of the past. The Egyptians used to entomb the living with the dead, I think. My throat tightens, and my limbs throw me out of my bed before I even realize. I stumble forward like a newborn calf, my chest heaving with effort as I fight off shadows and storm clouds, and the shackles of my disheveled linen and aimless feelings of guilt. I curve my fingers up underneath my windowpane and push it up, as far as it will go.

Cool air, and the scent of fresh air and rain. Petrichor, you told me, once. It blows against my wet skin, caresses my naked body and cools the heated dampness of my flesh. I close my eyes; breathe in, and then out, in, and out again in a shuddering sigh. The kind that makes your whole body tremble, top to toe. Rain drums its fingers gently on my face, sharp and cool and vigorous, washing off hot tears and stale sweat. I can hear the outside world now, the hum of cars, and the occasional siren, and seagulls in the distance. I can feel the wind, softly rustling my hair like the leaves on my da's great oak tree back home; caressing my skin the way I know you would, if you still could.

And you do. In the gray-blue balance between light and dark, somewhere between lucidity and dreaming, where time is yellow like honey, it is possible for you to stand by my side. I feel you next to me, as you always will be, in the night, when it rains.

I stand there until the sun starts to rise and the rain falters, and the world wakes. And I wake. Alive.

I feel you next to me,
as you always will be,
in the night, when it rains.

Crossed Lines

Sy Brand

I loved the rain
when I was alive, loved how
the water would hug me like you
from all sides, with sodden clothes,
how we'd be forced closer,
closer to hear over the drops'
incessant rush to Earth and you said
you loved it too—that's why
I sent you this storm, but
now you seem sad
and restless. Were you pretending?
Or does it remind you of me?

It's Winter in Edinburgh

Sy Brand

I loved the rain
when it was warm, when
I could still bear to go
outside, when energy
was a concept I understood, not
some absurd dream-memory;
now it's dark,
it's always dark, and I'm sure
the rain misses the sun
as much as I do, so now
I wait till the Earth shifts
so the light can shine back
off the morning mist
in the time of rainbows.

Rain
Cleaver

Sy Brand

I loved the rain
before we found it seeping
into our joists, rotting
our floor to give
underfoot; there's nothing stable
left in this house, now what gave us
comfort makes blood
rush in the dead of night
as we fail to sleep
in separate beds.

Hydrophobia

Elizabeth Ruth Deyro

Every so often, I would imitate the rain: tears crashing against
pavement, hoping they seep into the earth and fade
away. Instead tears dampen the ground
until puddle becomes flood and flood learns to be a hurricane
strong enough to drown
my cries and I crave   I still crave
for a wishful embrace, lovingly
suffocating.

When Girls Learn to Laugh

Elizabeth Ruth Deyro

—to Iya

bright-eyed
honeysuckle over-
exposed to the sting of sunlight, always
offering parts of herself
to strangers; to laugh
is to be kind, she thought—a child
to parents blinded by the hum-
drum noise of this polluted city
populated by polluted minds.
Sunchild is what I call her:
calling weather forecast as signs
from the stars while I feigned
interest about how drizzle in the middle
of summer means there is hope
for me to heal. I hear her
rave about being *one of the boys*: the kind
young girls thought set them apart
when they were better off
apart from these prepubescent boys
with growing hunger
for flesh and
bone.

One Wednesday afternoon in the August blaze,
she came up to me, her grin cutting
across her face. *I was one of the boys again*
at school, I finally did it: earned
a spot in their assemblage.

I remember wanting to cry
when she told the story about the boy
from her class who proudly said
he wanted to be a rapist and everyone laughed.
I hear a ringing in my ears as the word escapes
my sister's mouth and she explained it was a joke
the crowd loved, even her teacher—a woman
who must have been at my sister's place
once in her younger life. But instead she said
ang laki naman ng pangarap mo, as if it were valid
to boast about wanting to rip women apart.
I wanted to chase after her, remind her
of how dangerous a young male could be,
remind her that words are never truly
empty, not as much as what I feel when my sister
asked me to keep a secret, and I swore
without thinking twice, only to find out that
this boy—a ticking time bomb at age twelve—
is whom she has been staying
up all night thinking about. I am left
to wonder just how much of my old self
she inherited, and why she had to get this fondness
for damage, this obsession with cruel
people, of all the things she could have taken.

Later that night, I told mother about the young boy's threat,
begged her to say something, to save my sister, to rage
for the girls inside those four walls, but worry did not cross
her face. *It must have been a joke*, she said, and I've lived long
enough to know that it is synonymous to *Boys will be boys*,
and memories of my mother crying after she found out
she'd been cheated on more times than she's been loved,

only to forgive and pretend to forget for a decade more
flashed right in front of my eyes. The ringing
in my ears grew louder, and I told my sister that I will
speak with the school administration instead, tell them
that they've been breeding rapists right under their nose,
and my sister called me vexing, said she hated a tattletale just
as her friends do, that silence
should be my new virtue, and suddenly
I see her on the floor of the restroom at the far back
of their godforsaken Catholic school, her back bare
against begrimed ceramic tiles, her hands restrained,
mouth forced shut as she tries to scream
for her life, her peace to be restored, her sanity back
intact while bodies she used to trust
hover above hers. Suddenly I hear my mother say *Boys*
will be boys and I feel her close her eyes
and the restroom door. Suddenly I hear my sister's teacher
congratulate the boys from her advisory class for realizing
their dream to split a woman's body in half. Suddenly
everyone is laughing at the joke except for me. Suddenly
I became the joke—I, and the way I try
to fight something carved in our very bones.
I cupped my ears and only when I see
my hands soaked in scarlet does the ringing stop.

a Drop,
a Flood

Eleanor Capaldi

I slept all day again. Every intention had been set to turn back the clock, but 2 a.m. became 3 a.m. became 4, and the time fell away, sun setting as I was rising. Tomorrow, I'll fix it tomorrow. The threshold to the next day was too close now. The clocks change tomorrow. What does it mean this time, do I lose an hour, gain an hour . . . I think, I lose.

I've gotten into the habit of dusk walks. It's a stretch of the legs. Something you used to do after dinner, or afternoons after you'd been sitting by the pool all day with your family on holiday, hugged by heat so different to our own at home.

I haven't seen bright sunlight in . . . is it weeks now, or months . . . I don't know anymore. But disorientation is what I've been after. The rain tiptoes round the windowpane. I risk putting a hand by the window and let a little sphere of water sit on my finger. This water has traveled further than me. Which ocean did you disappear from? Are you really a microbead, someone's long-forgotten glitter, or the spray of a wave that crashed a million miles away, come to rest, with me?

Raindrops are to my nights what robins are to the day. A welcome sight when they arrive, marking territory, punctuating the expanse with a song. The neighbor's houses look like fabric stretched over the round head of a pin through the droplet, shrunk by perspective. If only I could put my problems inside the droplet and let it slide away and be absorbed into the earth. I sit as if it's a bird resting with me, like I daren't want to jar it, my piece of magic that makes everything look different. I imagine her face in the raindrop. Distorted, sharp edges softening against the crescents. Still, perfect. Which makes the bit inside that's not really your heart but somewhere near it, somewhere like it, curl into itself and start calling out to you again. Like when you roll your fingers into your palm until the nails begin to dig, really dig, into your own hands so it hurts.

Outside the rainfall becomes a steady rush, but I keep my hand steady, and let the rain sit with me a bit longer.

I
imagine
her face in
the raindrop

drown (me)

Montana Leigh Jackson

i have always
been in love with the types of weather
that exist to fill the spaces
around me; the sight of snow
or rain
or lightning strikes that flood
not only the sky
but my head with light—
nothing less than blessings to me.

if i could i would fold myself
into a rainstorm and never
come out—every droplet:
a protective cover.
every threat of flood:
a safety net.
each murmur
or whisper
or ear-shattering rumble of thunder:
a plea for me to

come home.

Leaving
Juliette

Eilidh G Clark

Juliette watches silently as bullets of hail bounce on the airplane's wing. The early morning's offering of sunshine that she'd been so relieved to wake up to is now hidden behind scribbles of charcoal clouds and a heavy sky. She grumbles obscenities under her breath. Beside her, Isobel sleeps silently.

Twenty minutes later than scheduled, the blinking seat belt signs suggests they are about to leave. There are murmurs around the cabin; clicking of belts and rustling of newspapers. Juliette turns her head toward Isobel, whose flickering eye-lids border between sleep and awake. She shushes her back to sleep. Isobel shivers, and her pale hand slides from a gap in her tartan shawl and pulls the garment up to her neck; she purses her lips, frowns, then rests her head on the back of her seat.

As soon as the airplane is in the sky, the cabin fills with chitter-chatter and the smell of fresh coffee. Juliette sucks on a mint imperial, clattering it around her dentures until her ears pop. The tea trolley rattles past with a chorus of, "Any hot drinks or snacks? Anything from the bar?"

A middle-aged woman in PVC trousers and a pink pon-cho leans across the aisle toward Juliette. "I think Sleeping Beauty there is needing a wee espresso."

"I'm sorry?" Juliette says.

"Well, it's such a short flight. We're hardly up before we're back down again." She flicks her hair over her shoulder. "Be-sides, the sun's splitting the trees down there in Dublin. You don't want your woman there to be missing out on a beautiful landing, now do you?"

"My woman?"

"Your friend, your sister, your missus, whatever, I'm just

saying, there's a spectacle to behold down there in the autumn."

And doesn't Juliette know it. Autumn, as it happens, is a precious time of year. She rests her head on Isobel's shoulder and closes her eyes.

She'd met Isobel in autumn of 1989. Juliette was on a return flight from Glasgow following four days at a horticultural course in the botanic gardens. She felt tired and her muscles ached from digging and stretching. Isobel had been sitting across the aisle with a group of friends, some of which were being loud and obnoxious. Juliette had noticed the young woman immediately and thought she must have the Celtic blood in her veins to be blessed with hair of the color of fire. She caught Red Head's eye and gave her an appreciative nod. The woman flashed her a quizzical look and turned back to her group. Juliette picked up her battered copy of Orlando and turned away from the hubbub.

Fifteen minutes before landing, her reading was disturbed by the sound of raised voices. She lowered her book and sat up straight to see what was going on. A man in a pinstriped suit four seats in front her was jabbing a finger toward the group of friends. His face was red and twisted in anger. From among the jumble of words being thrown back and forth across the aisle, she managed to pick out "queer" and "gay boys." Her shoulders tightened, and she dropped Orlando onto the empty seat. She unclipped her seat belt with trembling fingers and was about to rush to the boy's defense when two cabin crew swept down the aisle to defuse the situation. Juliette sat back in her seat, closed her eyes, and blew out a breath. Her heart was racing.

Red Head tapped Juliette on the shoulder.

"Are you alright?"

"I will be," Juliette replied.

"Do you mind?" She nodded toward the empty seat.

Juliette lifted her book. "Be my guest."

The seat belt sign lit up, and both women fiddled with their straps until they were locked in.

"I can't believe people still act like that," Juliette said, still stiff with anger.

"I know. I'm so embarrassed," Red Head said. "I told them not to be so, you know, out there in front of other people." She shook her head.

"Oh no." Juliette blushed. "I was referring to him there," she said in a raised voice, pointing at the man in the suit, who was now arguing with his wife.

Red Head cowered into her seat. "I guess I'm just envious. I wish I had the courage to be so bold."

They sat in silence for the next ten minutes. Juliette fidgeted in her seat, while Red Head twirled a strand of hair around her finger and whistled under her breath.

"I'm Isobel, by the way." Red Head turned so that their faces were close; Juliette felt her warm breath.

"Juliette," she answered; the skin of their arms brushed slightly. "Are you Scottish?"

"Can't you tell?" Isobel smirked.

"You don't belong to Glasgow, that's for sure."

"As a matter of fact, I do."

"Really?"

"Student accent, I guess."

"I see. What are you studying, Isobel?"

"I was studying public health. Just finished."

"Doctor?"

"Aye."

"Well done."

The airplane dipped its left wing to turn and then begin its descent.

"Have you been to Dublin before?" Juliette asked.

"First time, but I've been told if the weather's clear it's a beautiful landing."

"That it is." She sat back. "Take a look."

Isobel leaned over Juliette's lap. A ringlet of red hair fell on Juliette's bottle-green blouse, and the contrast was striking.

"You'll be seeing Killiney Bay about now," Juliette said, "and beyond that, the glorious Wicklow Mountains."

"Wow. Would you look at the colors of those trees." Isobel turned to face Juliette with wild blue eyes. "Do you want to see?"

"I've seen them a hundred times."

"It's like the mountains have captured a rainbow."

"I like to imagine that every tree and every bush, and all the grass and flowers hold the entire summer inside of them, then in the autumn it all spills out."

"Stunning."

For a second, their eyes locked. Juliette held her breath, and although the blood rushed through her veins, there was a feeling of familiarity, like she'd been reunited with a long-lost lover.

"Thank you for this." Isobel squeezed Juliette's hand gently before reaching forward one last time and filling the window with hair the color of fire.

Juliette could see in her mind's eye the Japanese larch, the pines and the spruce, stretched up to the sky and swaying from side to side, back and forth, sweeping brush strokes in the clouds. From up here, she could almost see the forest breathe.

"I hope you don't think I'm being too forward, but can I see you again?" Isobel asked as the airplane bumped to the ground. "I'm here for a week and I just thought, seeing as you're local . . . "

"What gave you the impression I'm local?"

"It's the accent, I just . . . "

"You're right, I'm just playing around with you."

"So, do you fancy . . . "

"I'm free on Wednesday evening if you are." Juliette laughed and felt giddy.

"I'll make myself free." Isobel grinned.

"Okay. Meet me in John Kavanagh's on Prospect Square. Is seven o'clock okay?"

"Aye."

Juliette wore a pair of pin tuck trousers and a black polo neck. She waited at the bar, sipping Malibu and pineapple through a straw and tapping her feet to "Never Too Late" by Kylie Minogue. A few minutes later, the young doctor arrived. She looked younger than Juliette remembered and dressed casually in double denim with green Doc Martens and matching earrings. The long red curls that had first caught Juliette's eye were tied into a ponytail. Juliette immediately felt her age. But later that night, as they stood in an alleyway to avoid the rain, Isobel leaned forward and kissed Juliette. It was the first time she'd been kissed like that.

Juliette pulls the inflight magazine from the seat pocket and flicks through its glossy pages; adverts, adverts, and more of the same.

"Excuse me, dear." A voice interrupts her thoughts. A heavily made-up face leans toward her with red lips pulled into a smile revealing straight white teeth.

Juliette raises her eyes.

"Would you like a hot beverage? Tea, coffee . . . "

"Someone was here just ten minutes ago," Juliette says. "No thank you."

"And for your daughter?" Juliette feels a stab in her chest.

"She's asleep."

"Yes. But . . . "

"Nothing for either of us. Thank you."

"If you change your mind, dear . . . " She points at a button above the seat. "Just press this one."

Juliette nods and raises the magazine to cover her flushed cheeks. If it isn't bad enough being insulted with the title of "dear," being mistaken for Isobel's mother is deplorable.

The age gap hadn't been so obvious at the start; Juliette had just turned forty and her premenopausal body was still trim with a flicker of youthfulness. Isobel on the other hand was twenty-one and glowed. Since their first encounter, they'd kept in contact with each other by telephone at least once a day, if not twice. Juliette was completely consumed with love, and according to Isobel, the feeling was mutual. Yet Juliette was reluctant to commit to a relationship, never mind that type of relationship. She assumed, as one would, that Isobel was just dipping her toes in the water and would soon get bored with the lifestyle of a middle-aged woman, never mind the gossip. But Isobel didn't refrain from trying. Nevertheless,

Juliette kept her lover at a distance for ten whole years, meaning both women would travel between Glasgow and Dublin at the weekends, birthdays, and holidays.

"Do you remember that first flight?" Isobel asked her on one of those sleepless rainy nights as they lay in bed together.

"Of course, I do," Juliette said, stretching her tired limbs.

"I think about it every time I fly here," Isobel said. "I almost kissed you on that flight. I'd never felt so drawn to anyone like that before."

"I felt like I'd found you after years of looking," Juliette breathed into her ear.

"You old romantic." Isobel kissed her. "But isn't it about time we began making new memories? Besides, I'm exhausted."

The flights to and from Glasgow stopped in the first autumn of the millennium. And when Isobel moved in, not a word of gossip passed from the lips of the villagers. Assuming that unlucky-in-love Juliette was past her mothering years and was now a spinster, what else could the young Isobel be but the spinster's lodger. After all, she'd been visiting as a "friend" for ten years. This suited Isobel well, although it irritated Juliette, but Isobel's new career as a family practitioner and the sole female doctor in the practice meant absolute discretion. They set up separate bedrooms in Juliette's two-bed bungalow, in case, as Isobel pointed out, of a surprise visitor or people passing by the back window. But Juliette corrected her, saying that whenever they were in bed together, the curtains were firmly closed. And as for the people passing the back window, that would only be the village gardener, Juliette herself.

For most of the time, their fabricated life wasn't an issue; the back-room door stayed closed, the room gathering dust, and their relationship shone. Then one afternoon, Juliette was pruning Mrs. Candleberry's Arthur Bell roses, when the lady herself appeared in the garden with a tray carrying two glasses of Pimm's.

"So, tell me about your young doctor friend," Mrs. Candleberry said, putting the tray on the table. She pulled out a chair and patted it. "Join me for a refreshment."

"Isobel." Juliette took a handkerchief from the pocket of her shirt and mopped her brow. "What about her?"

"Well, what's she like to live with? Has she got a man-friend?" She put her hand to the side of her mouth and whispered, "I hear she's friendly with Doctor Luton."

"Doctor Luton?"

"He's new to the practice. A handsome young Australian man."

"She hasn't mentioned him." Juliette dug her fingernails into the palm of her hand, leaving a line of half-moons.

"Well, I'm sure two attractive doctors don't need any help from us old hens, but it wouldn't hurt to give your little friend a nudge?"

Juliette almost choked on an ice cube.

"Although," she continued, "I'm sure you don't want to lose a good lodger. It must be nice to have the company of a younger woman in the house."

"Nice. Yes."

"And the rent, of course. Such a shame to have to manage on your own without a . . . "

"I manage just fine, Mrs. Candleberry."

"I was just saying to Hilda and Betty at the church hall this morning that Isobel could almost be mistaken for your daughter."

"My . . . "

"There's such a likeness, dear," she went on, "over the mouth and . . . " Her voice was drowned out by the scraping of Juliette's chair on the concrete. She marched back to the roses.

"I've got to get on, Mrs. Candleberry," she shouted over her shoulder. "Mr. Dingle is expecting me in half an hour." But she raced home that afternoon, stripped off her grubby clothes, and stood in front of the mirror. Then she cried, all the feelings of doubt returning to her mind.

Isobel shrugged it off later that evening. "There's hardly a line on your face," she said, tucking a stand of brown hair behind Juliette's ear and brushing her lips over her earlobe. "And besides, I would be lucky to look anything like you. You're stunning."

"But one day soon I'm going to be an old lady and you, you'll be in your prime." Juliette shrugged. "And then you'll leave me."

"Why would I leave you?"

And for the next decade their flights remained grounded, and together they celebrated each new wrinkle, cried over ailments, and watched each other grow. But sometimes, on a dark and rainy night, Juliette would lie awake wondering when it would all end.

The plane judders and the seat belt sign lights up again. Juliette gently lifts Isobel's shawl and checks that her belt is firmly in place, then checks her own. She looks at her watch; they've been in the air for twenty minutes now, which means there are only thirty-seven minutes to go. She listens to Isobel breathe while all around her teacups rattle on saucers and a couple shout at a child. At the back of the airplane someone is crying. The cabin girl that earlier called her dear staggers from left to right as she makes her way to her own seat by the door. Juliette considers pushing the little button above her head, then scolds herself for thinking bad thoughts. Suddenly the airplane dips. There are wide eyes and a collective gasp, and someone screams for God. Juliette swings her arm toward Isobel, searching for her hand, and Isobel wakes. She struggles to free her arms from her shawl but, of course, she's held tightly by her seat belt.

"What the—"

The airplane settles, followed by an apology over the intercom.

"It's okay." Juliette twists to face Isobel, who is thrashing around, red-faced. She puts her two hands on Isobel's face and turns it toward her own. Isobel stops writhing and looks at Juliette. Their eyes lock. Juliette breathes sharply and holds her breath. She searches those familiar eyes, still as blue as the sky after a storm. Isobel smiles; a dimple that's grown deeper with age bends as her lips stretch.

"Hey, my love." Juliette's heart quickens. "It's me, Juliette." She reaches out and takes Isobel's hands.

Isobel clears her throat. "Do you have an appointment, dear?" She shakes Juliette's hands away and starts pulling things from the seat pocket and dropping them on the floor. "I can't seem to find my diary. What did you say your name was?"

Juliette feels a familiar gnawing of disappointment, but she blinks it away. "I'm not here to see a doctor, I'm here to see you."

Isobel frowns and sits back in her seat. "Are we on a bus?"

Juliette pulls the shade down.

"We're on an airplane to Dublin."

"Where's Juliette? What have you done with Juliette?" She begins tugging on her seat belt.

"I'm here—"

"Stop this bus!" Isobel shouts at the top of her voice.

"Isobel . . ."

"Help! I'm being held hostage!"

Juliette unclips her seat belt and stands up. She holds Isobel by the shoulders.

"Is everything alright?" A bald head pops up from the seat in front.

"Ma'am." Juliette's favorite steward stands in the aisle. "Is everything alright?"

"Everything is fine." Juliette puts her arm out to warn the steward to stay back. "She's . . . "

"Are you here for an appointment, dear?" Isobel smiles at the steward.

"She's radio rental." A little blonde girl with pretend tattoos drapes her arms over Juliette's head rest.

"Don't be so rude," Juliette snaps, then turns to the steward. "She's just confused."

They thought it was fatigue at first, what with the extra shifts she'd been covering due to Dr. O'Brian's pregnancy.

"You can't just diagnose yourself with exhaustion, then go in to work on a Saturday," Juliette snapped after finding an egg bouncing in a dry saucepan on the kitchen hob. "You need to take time off."

"I can't. Deloris is as sick as a dog with this wee one, and besides, there's no one else to cover for her."

"Fair enough, but remember you'll have to finish early on Monday, you've got a hospital appointment to get that left leg looked at again."

"My left leg?" Isobel looked puzzled.

"The trapped nerve . . . "

"Aye, right enough," she said, limping out of the room.

But Isobel didn't finish early that Monday, or the following Monday, and as the weeks went by, Juliette lost count of the times she'd canceled and rearranged appointments. But it was six months later when things came to a head.

Juliette was in the kitchen organizing sandwiches onto serving trays. They were expecting a dozen friends over in the evening to celebrate their upcoming twentieth anniversary.

Isobel burst into the kitchen with arms full of shopping bags.

"Is the cake in the car?" Juliette asked.

"Cake?" Isobel dropped the bags at her feet.

"The anniversary . . . " Juliette began.

A tin of dog food rolled from one of the bags and landed near Juliette's feet. She picked it up and looked at Isobel. The confusion on her face sent shivers down Juliette's spine.

"We don't have a dog, do we?" Isobel said softly.

"We don't." Juliette pulled out a kitchen chair and took Isobel's hand. "Sit down, love."

Isobel was trembling.

After the diagnosis Isobel took sick leave from work and began reading prolifically. Being a doctor, she had access to the best medical books on early onset dementia. She collected them all and shut herself in the second bedroom and spent weeks poring over them. Then one day, out of the blue, she packed the books into a large cardboard box and took them to the office. Juliette waited in the car.

"Do you want to go on a road trip?" Isobel asked when she returned.

"Today?" Juliette asked.

"Why not. I want to make up for forgetting our . . . " She held her mouth open, as if waiting for the word to drop out.

"Anniversary?" Juliette lifted her eyebrows.

"Aye, that. I feel so disconnected from everything." Isobel blushed. "Shall we?"

"Where do you want to go?"

"Wicklow Mountains."

So, approximately three weeks after their twentieth anniversary, they laid their sleeping bags on the ground on top of a thick bed of moss and fallen pine needles at the foot of Wicklow Mountains.

"Who needs a mattress?" Juliette said and breathed deeply. The forest smelled of damp mulch and burning firewood.

Isobel tucked a cushion under her head. "We should have done this years ago," she said, looking up at the trees swishing in the breeze. "Look"—she pointed—"Fred Astaire and Ginger Rodgers!"

Juliette looked up to see two Scots pines bent toward one another in a romantic embrace.

Isobel turned to Juliette. "Thank you for twenty years of good memories."

"And here's to making new ones," Juliette replied.

"Memory might not be my strong point though." Isobel sighed.

"I'm sure it won't be as bad as you think."

"Oh, Juliette. We need to talk."

Isobel sat up and crossed her legs.

"I know you're worried, my love. I am too." Juliette brushed the palm of her hand over Isobel's cheek. "But if things get difficult, I'll look after you."

Isobel turned to face Juliette. "Promise me you'll bring me here every year on our anniversary."

"Of course."

"Even if I forget you, I think this is the place that will bring it all back."

Juliette reached over and held her hand. She choked back her tears.

"Will you collect me from Glasgow." Isobel's blue eyes were heavy and full.

Juliette sat up. "What?"

"I'm going back to Scotland. Everything's arranged."

"No. You can't." Juliette felt her body trembling. That familiar feeling that had kept her awake for so many nights. "You're leaving?"

"I'm setting you free."

Juliette feels the pressure change in the cabin as the airplane begins its descent. There's the usual hustle and bustle before landing; bags being stowed in overhead lockers; seats being put back in upright positions; last minute queues at the toilets. Isobel fiddles with the air-conditioning above her head; it blows strands of red hair over her face and she laughs.

"Isobel." Juliette whispers so as not to alarm her. "Do you want look outside?" She pulls the window blind up fully.

Slowly, Isobel reaches over and looks out. "No, no, no!" she shouts. "I think we're falling!"

"Oh no, darling, I promise you we're not." Juliette takes her hand. "Look, we're flying over Killiney Bay."

Isobel edges closer, her eyes widening. Suddenly, she

presses her finger on the window. "Aha!" she says. "Can you see that rainbow? That's where I'll find my Juliette."

Juliette smiles and nods.

The forest floor is dappled with sunlight. Long lingering licks of amber coat the leaves and branches. Isobel sits in the car while Juliette unpacks. She tries to ignore the ache in her heart while she sets about re-creating the past. She lays out two sleeping bags on the blanket of thick green moss, and two cushions. Beside each she places a bottle of water and a bag of mixed nuts. Even though they'd returned to this exact spot for the last ten years, she checks for their initials on the bark of the spruce that they'd carved five years ago.

"I'll never stop trying," she says, tracing her finger over the rough bark.

Before she fetches Isobel from the car, she stands for a moment and breathes the cool damp air. High above her, Fred and Ginger stand still, like strangers.

Contributors

Lola Gaztañaga Baggen is a multinational antinationalist polyglot with a penchant for black clothes, colorful scarves, and anything folklore. Having lived in the wonderfully gothic Edinburgh for going on three years now, she takes full inspiration to write the dark, magical, and disturbed, but a childhood spent in Holland and Spain means she also specializes in dyke reviews and siesta manuals.

Sy Brand is a queer nonbinary person living in Edinburgh, Scotland. They write through the haze of cat-/child-induced sleep deprivation to try and make sense of gender, relationships, and ADHD. You can find them at @TartanLlama on Twitter and their publications at https://sybrand.ink.

Eleanor Capaldi is a writer and director based in Scotland. She has been published by *Gutter Magazine*, *The Interpreter's House*, and *The Skinned Knee Collective* and in anthologies including *Queering the Map of Glasgow* (Knight Errant Press), *Beyond Boundaries* (European Championships Cultural Commission), and *Reel to Rattling Reel* (Cranachan). Her journalism has appeared in *DIVA Magazine*, *VICE*, *Munchies*, and *The Skinny* and for Glasgow Film Theatre. Short films *Pull* (2017) and *Glue* (2019) have screened in competition at the Scottish Queer International Film Festival and more.

Eilidh G Clark is a writer and poet who lives in Killin in Stirlingshire, Scotland. Eilidh's work has been published in print and online with publishers such as *Capsule Stories*, Fairlight Books, and *The Ogilvie*. In 2019, she was awarded second place in the Scottish Mental Health Arts Festival for her short story

"Message in a Bottle." She was also shortlisted for the Crossing the Tees festival for her short story "Kit House." You can find more of Eilidh's work at www.egclark.com.

Elizabeth Ruth Deyro is a journalist, poet, literary editor, and feminist from the Philippines. She has a BA in communication arts from the University of the Philippines Los Baños, specializing in media studies and creative writing. She is a Pushcart Prize nominee. Her literary work has appeared or is forthcoming in *Rust + Moth*, *Hypertrophic Literary*, *Porridge Magazine*, *Ache Magazine*, and *The Poetry Annals*, among others. She founded *The Brown Orient*, published *RECLAIM: An Anthology of Women's Poetry*, volunteers at Gantala Press, and is a columnist at *Half Mystic*.

Alolika A. Dutta is an eighteen-year-old author and poet based in Bombay, India. Most of her work surrounds politics, culture, and identity. Her work can be found in *Yellow Medicine Review*, *Away With Words*, *Coldnoon*, *Unread*, and so on.

Larry Griggs holds a BFA in English from the University of West Georgia. He works as a writing tutor and substitute teacher in his hometown. When he isn't reading or writing, he is taking care of the many animals his significant other brings home. His debut novel *All Apart of the Chaos* is available on Amazon.

James Croal Jackson (he/him) has a chapbook, *The Frayed Edge of Memory* (Writing Knights Press, 2017), and po-

---

ems in *Pacifica, Reservoir,* and *Rattle.* He edits *The Mantle Poetry* (themantlepoetry.com). Currently, he works in the film industry in Pittsburgh. You can find him online at jimjakk.com.

Cassia Hameline is a PhD student in creative nonfiction at the University of North Texas. Her work has been published by or is forthcoming in *Blanket Sea, The Fix, Cosmonauts Avenue, Utterance,* and elsewhere. She lives in Denton, Texas, where you can usually find her in the woods with her dog, Moab.

Tianna G. Hansen has been writing her whole life. She is the founder and editor-in-chief of Rhythm & Bones Press, focused on trauma-turned-art. Much of her work focuses on living with trauma and empowerment. Her published work can be found at creativetianna.com. Follow her on Twitter at @tiannag92.

Karin Hedetniemi writes essays about nature, inspiration, and being human. Her work has appeared in *Sky Island Journal* and *Pomme Journal.* Karin originally studied humanities, then followed a winding path to nonprofit management in environmental education. Now dedicated to new life experiences, she recently walked two Camino pilgrimage trails in Spain. Her home in Victoria, British Columbia, is filled with books on travel, gardening, spirituality, and birds and a lifetime of notes evolving into stories. You can read some of them on her website AGoldenHour.com.

Juleigh Howard-Hobson has poetry published in *Mooky-chick*, *Valparaiso Poetry Review*, *Dreams & Nightmares*, *Ghost City Review*, *Autumn Sky Poetry Daily*, *The Lyric*, *Able Muse*, *Coffin Bell*, *Lift Every Voice* (Kissing Dynamite), *Poem*, *Revised* (Marion Street Press), *Birds Fall Quiet in the Mechanical Sea* (Great Weather for Media), and many other places. She is an urban dropout, living off-grid in the middle of rural nowhere, USA. She has been nominated for the Pushcart Prize, The Best of the Net, and the Rhysling Award. Find her at @PoetForest on Twitter.

Montana Leigh Jackson is a communication studies student in Montreal, Quebec. Her work has been featured in *semicolon* and *Turnpike Magazine*. She finds peace amongst words and within thunderstorms.

Isabella J Mansfield writes about the many faces of anxiety, body image, intimacy, and the human condition. She favors free-verse poetry over traditional poetry "rules," but can sometimes be found writing the occasional tanka, senryu, and haiku. Mansfield has performed at Oberon (Cambridge, Massachusetts) and Nambucca (London, UK), as well as many locations in and around Lansing, Michigan. Her poems have been featured by *Philosophical Idiot*, *The Wild Word*, *And So Yeah*, *Sad Girl Review*, and *Capsule Stories*, as well as in publications by PoetsIN, Augie's Bookshelf, and Rebel Mountain Press. In 2017, she was a Brittany Noakes Poetry Award semifinalist. She won the 2018 Mark Ritzenhein New Author Award. Finishing Line Press published her Pushcart Prize-nominated chapbook, *The Hollows of Bone*, in 2019. She lives in Howell, Michigan, with her family.

Niamh McNally is a twenty-four-year-old poet from Ireland whose writing focuses on the physicality of space and material within our everyday lives. She cocreated a student-led publication called *The Paperclip* in 2019 and was published in *Tulsa Review*. Being continuously inspired by the elements, Niamh agrees that lying in her warm bed, tucked up under the covers, and being kept awake by the unforgiving rain is where the imagination thrives and the poetry begins.

Benjamin Middendorf is a writer, despite all evidence to the contrary. He graduated from Concordia University, Nebraska (CUNE) with a BA in English, psychology, and gerontology. Some of his writing has previously appeared in *Potpourri*, CUNE's creative writing journal, and *The Sower*, CUNE's student-led newspaper. Benjamin currently works with the elderly and adults with disabilities in Lincoln, Nebraska, and continues to write fiction and poetry.

Ada Pelonia is a writer from the Philippines. Her work has appeared in *The Philippines Graphic, inQluded, 101 Words, The Brown Orient*, and elsewhere.

Kushal Poddar authored *The Circus Came to My Island* (Spare Change Press), *A Place for Your Ghost Animals* (Ripple Effect Publishing), *Understanding the Neighborhood* (Blank Rune Books), *Scratches Within* (Barbara Maat), *Kleptomaniac's Book of Unoriginal Poems* (Blank Rune Press), *Eternity Restoration Project: Selected and New Poems* (Hawakal Publishers), and *Herding My Thoughts to the Slaughterhouse: A Prequel* (Alien Buddha Press).

Fabrice Poussin teaches French and English at Shorter University. He is an author of novels and poetry, and his work has appeared in *Kestrel*, *Symposium*, *The Chimes*, and many other magazines. His photography has been published in *Front Porch Review* and *San Pedro River Review*, as well as other publications.

Lee Clark Zumpe, an entertainment columnist with *Tampa Bay Newspapers*, earned his bachelor's in English at the University of South Florida. He began writing poetry and fiction in the early 1990s. His work has regularly appeared in a variety of literary journals and genre magazines over the last two decades. Publication credits include *Tiferet*, *Zillah*, *The Ugly Tree*, *Modern Drunkard Magazine*, *Red Owl*, *Jones Av.*, *Main Street Rag*, *Space and Time*, *Mythic Delirium*, and *Weird Tales*. Lee lives on the west coast of Florida with his wife and daughter. Visit leeclarkzumpe.com.

I stand there until the sun starts to rise and the rain falters, and the world wakes.

And I wake. Alive.

Editorial Staff

Natasha Lioe, Founder and Publisher

Natasha Lioe graduated with a BA in narrative studies from University of Southern California. She's always had an affinity for words and stories and emotions. Her work has appeared in *Adsum Literary Magazine* and *Capsule Stories*, and she won the Edward B. Moses Creative Writing Competition in 2016. Her greatest strength is finding and focusing the pathos in an otherwise cold world, and she hopes to help humans tell their unique, compelling stories.

Carolina VonKampen, Publisher and Editor in Chief

Carolina VonKampen graduated with a BA in English and history from Concordia University, Nebraska and completed the University of Chicago's editing certificate program. She is available for hire as a freelance copyeditor and proofreader. Her writing has appeared in *So to Speak*'s blog, *FIVE:2:ONE*'s #thesideshow, *Moonchild Magazine*, and *Déraciné Magazine*. Her short story "Logan Paul Is Dead" was nominated by *Dream Pop Journal* for the 2018 Best of the Net. She writes book reviews and blog posts at carolinavonkampen.com, tweets about editing at @carolinamarie_v, and talks about books she's reading on Instagram at @carolinamariereads.

Submission
Guidelines

Capsule Stories **is a print literary magazine** published once every season. Our first issue was published on March 1, 2019, and we accept submissions year-round.

Become published in a literary magazine run by like-minded people. We have a penchant for pretty words, an affinity to the melancholy, and an undeniably time-ful aura. We believe that stories exist in a specific moment, and that that moment is what makes those stories unique.

What we're really looking for are stories that can touch the heart. Stories that come from the heart. Stories about love, identity, the self, the world, the human condition. Stories that show what living in this world as the human you are is like.

We accept short stories, poems, and remarkably written essays. For short stories and essays, we're interested in pieces under 3000 words. You may include up to five poems in a single poetry submission, and please send only one story or essay at a time. Please send previously unpublished work only, and only submit to one category at a time. Simultaneous submissions are okay, but please let us know if your submission is accepted elsewhere. Please include a brief third-person bio with your submission, and attach your submission in a Word document (no PDFs, please!).

You can email your submission to us at submissions@capsulestories.com.

Connect with us!
@CapsuleStories on Twitter and Facebook
@CapsuleStoriesMag on Instagram

CPSIA information can be obtained
at www.ICGtesting.com
Printed in the USA
BVHW092024080320
574407BV00004B/25

9 781734 324624